DOODLE ART ALLEY BOOKS

VOLUME 5

Samantha Snyder

Copyright © 2015 Doodle Art Alley.
All rights reserved.

Amazing Grace is available at special discounts when purchased in quantities for educational use, fundraising, or sales promotions. For more information, contact: info@akabooks.com

Cover images © 2015 by Doodle Art Alley.

ISBN-13: 978-0983918240
ISBN-10: 0983918244

This edition is published by aka Associates.
www.akabooks.com

Doodle Art Alley Books

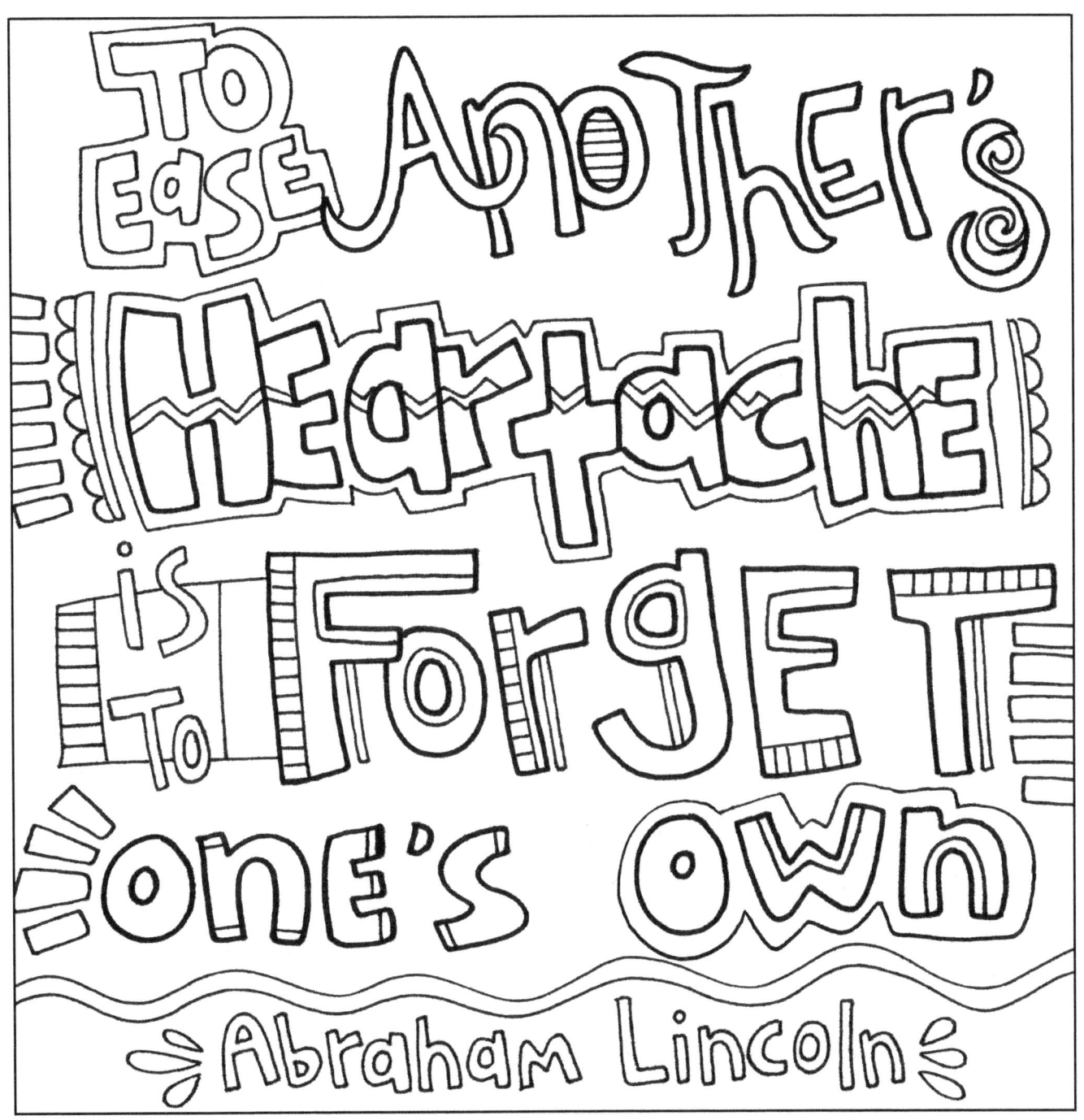

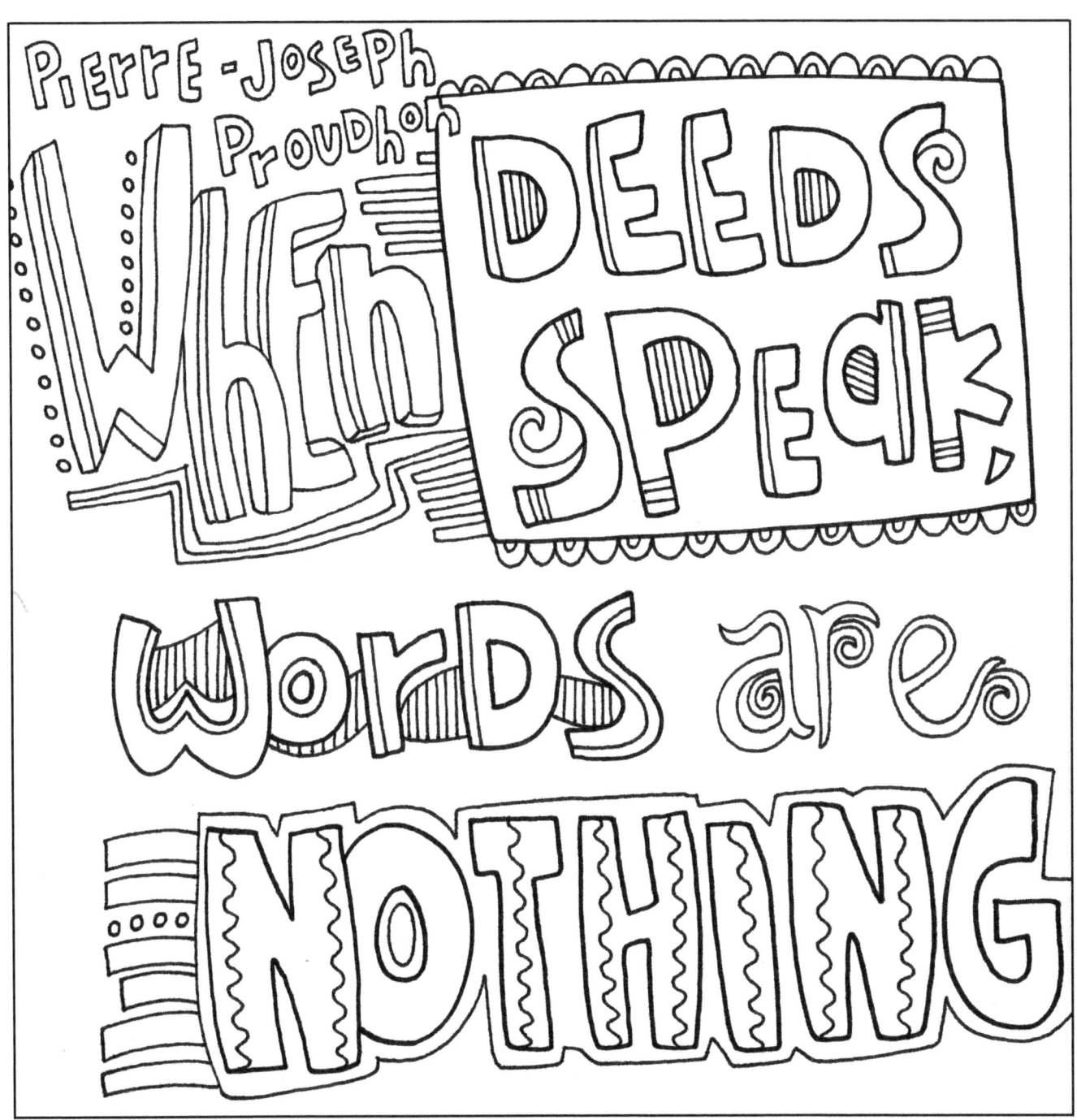

ABOUT DOODLE ART ALLEY

Samantha Snyder has been doodling her whole life. While teaching elementary school, she often drew up coloring pages and printables for her students and fellow teachers. She decided to start sharing her creations and in 2008, Doodle Art Alley was founded.

A quick glance at a doodle may show scribbles, random lines and shapes with no meaning or significance. However, with a little love and direction, these drawings have the potential to compete with some of the best artwork there is!

Doodle Art Alley is dedicated to giving those squiggly lines the proper credit they deserve. Who would have thought that such a small and simple idea could possess so much potential?

There are lots of fun doodle art activities, tips, and information to read through and enjoy. Visit www.doodle-art-alley.com for hundreds of exciting doodles.

Doodle Art Alley Books

www.ingramcontent.com/pod-product-compliance
Lightning Source LLC
Chambersburg PA
CBHW060517300426
44112CB00017B/2706